Joël Pourbaix

Homesickness Is a Forgotten Art

Translated by Donald Winkler

BookLand press

Published by BookLand Press
15 Allstate Parkway, Suite 600, Markham, Ontario L3R 5B4
www.booklandpress.com

Printed in Canada

Library and Archives Canada Cataloguing in Publication

Pourbaix, Joël
[Mal du pays est un art oublié. English]
Homesickness is a forgotten art / Joël Pourbaix; translated by Donald Winkler.

Translation of: Le mal du pays est un art oublié.
Poems.
Issued in print and electronic formats.
ISBN 978-1-77231-059-7 (softcover).--ISBN 978-1-77231-060-3 (EPUB).--
ISBN 978-1-77231-061-0 (PDF)

I. Winkler, Donald, translator II. Title. III. Title: Mal du pays est un art oublié. English.

PS8581.O87M3413 2018 C841'.54 C2017-907130-0
C2017-907131-9

Canada Council for the Arts Conseil des arts du Canada

ONTARIO ARTS COUNCIL
CONSEIL DES ARTS DE L'ONTARIO
an Ontario government agency
un organisme du gouvernement de l'Ontario

We acknowledge the financial support of the Government of Canada through the National Translation Program for Book Publishing, an initiative of the *Roadmap for Canada's Official Languages 2013-2018: Education, Immigration, Communities*, for our translation activities. We acknowledge the support of the Canada Council for the Arts, which last year invested $153 million to bring the arts to Canadians throughout the country. We acknowledge the support of the Ontario Arts Council (OAC), an agency of the Government of Ontario.

Table of Contents

Part 1
The Heretics of Paradise

No Promenade Is Simple | 11
My Friend Henri | 23
The Night of the Blind | 33
Mortal Endeavours | 45
Verticals One | 59

Part 2
The Ashes of Initiation

The Return of the Cliff | 73
On the Roads of Pontiac | 85
In the Caves of the Kingdom | 97
The Soul of the Fox | 109
The Fugitive from the Journey | 121
Verticals Two | 129

Part 1
The Heretics of Paradise

Oh I want so much to leave this world!
and yet so far from it
I wander, a flickering light
about God's tomb.

~ Else Lasker-Schüler

No Promenade Is Simple

Screeching birds and slamming doors, I'm wise to the public hubbub's tide gnawing away at the decorum of dawn. What's needy and real will rain down on hearts and heads. Come out from your hole, compose yourself, cull one more small reason to live for the hour, the day, the week, pick yourself up and walk. This commonplace miracle shuns me, I fix my eyes on the river's dark waters.

I'd like to believe in calm faces that honour a bridge without passing over it.

I make people out more clearly when they're drifting into the distance, their backs receding from view. A silhouette slipping away leaves a powdery trail in the failing night. Matter fondled by light still affirms its nakedness, the first shadows are wed to stones, betroth themselves to the rifts and grain of things, while the glad life of what's left behind vaunts a mineral bliss.

All through the morning's apocalypse, the earth keeps watch on the sky's last shreds.

People leaf through newspapers or gaze at steam that lifts from their cups. They don't ask themselves if they're happy. The café is their haven, timeworn rituals spin out the fragile fiat of a day yet to be lived. Yet an ember's fate is to be borne, transported, I hear muffled words, the odd prospect of investing meaning in what has none. Just one conversation alone risks transforming what is real. My instants of hope, like my heartbeats, are not mine to choose.

A beautiful face wafts its silence to the end of the table.

A girl with pierced eyelids sits before me. Her soul hangs by a thread round her neck, a frog preens beneath her fingers, she shows it off, see, lit from within like an icon. But she turns her head away, her mind strays once more to her array of what's been lost, and to the empty gaps lipless lowlifes have left in their wake. Time is of no help at all, unpunished crimes pelt down on the hour to come.

It's too easy for me to retreat before a shielding of heavy sorrow, while just flagging its flaws.

Who's chained up, who's free, what help for a weak link when we are broken, taking flight, leaping black holes from one street to the next. I so much wanted to endow her with words, not those that save the world or proclaim its end, but those that would have you walk on reality's waters. Every day that passes is due its turf, its stories tendered and received where nothing grows.

She saw in me that to which I could not confess: the geography of my discontent.

The dandies in desperate straits disguise their blindness and defer to a later date the landslide even now sweeping us away. Here, the dead weight of the fearful who are lost in a wash of rumour. There, fuelled on mood pills for mental well-being, high livers and their discreet despair. The wrath at having been one of their number, the fear of being so again.

Unending, life's humdrum routine gnaws away at my weak-kneed gait.

The inconceivably glossy buds, the bare arms, the bare legs, May's warmth and its redolence of flesh. I try to brave the allure of being alive, find myself nebulous, free of pain and with no future. All conjurations are vain. I'm a dark parchment in a wood of mirrors. Inklings of ease are but a tiny wrinkle on bedlam's endless tract of skin.

A current of air drifts into my head, loved faces bid me again farewell.

My stroll tails off, face to face with a boldly lettered signpost: *You are here.* The blunt message drops sites and paths into a senseless void. My raptures are micro-managed. No need to be an imposter now to practise deception, you kill off a dozen thoughts per day, more than enough. This age obsessed with coherence scorns unstudied inspiration, revelations are weapons banned from use. There once was a time when to stray was not to be lost.

To roam is as rare as the sound of a map unfolding.

My cloistered thought grips humanity in its vise, indexing its disasters. The martyrs' stake, great bonfires and autos-da-fé lick at my sleepless exegetic nights. Gods abound, and we are dogged by yesteryear's savagery. There's no dearth of scapegoats, to the delight of the voyeurs in their seats; I hew to no herd, yet the stench of abattoirs haunts me.

Cry out for desperate measures, and the living murmur on, but are unheard.

The luxury, at trifling cost, of feeling real, involved, of being more and ever more. Look on a picture, it becomes two. Tear it, it turns into four. Discuss it, and countless scraps of confetti signal a flawless sky. They don't even try to spawn dreams any more, it's me they dream, they thrive, their cup overflows. Can you in any way call it a victory, to undo ennui? The world is depraved that foists on our dreams the burden of fulfilment.

The slave's greatest worth lies not in compliance but in his longings.

Ruins and resurrections were still the order of the day at the dawn of this millennium. The hidden conduits for decoded truths shed light on our wandering in the kingdom of the blind. The horizon has since pursed tight its lips, no need for a precipice to lend free-fall a name, nothing is left that will do so. All-seeing, I am untouchable, opaque, an isle on the raging waves. The protocols of happiness shielded me for a time from the vagaries of life. The protocols of gloom are much the same, here life lies down beneath proud shells, sand-silted.

Beyond oneself, the deluge, the wearied terrible routine.

After so many years inhabited by mirages, the vanished now huddle round me. What has become of them? I can't just put them to death along with the fleeting happy days, the wild and pious rites that spanned my life. I keep on going, knowing the world's still full of faces seared by the sun, drinking water from ditches. No one arrives to reach out a hand to walking shadows.

To peer over the edge of oneself has been always taboo.

My Friend Henri

It's unseemly, disgraceful, to be wretched in public. The man extended on musty cardboard reaches out a blackened hand before pulling it back behind a blind of feathers and rags. Compassion is a passing fancy that quickly fades. He grabs hold of a torn bag, lifts a green bottle, trembling, to his lips. Between the loners intent on blessing the bread of helplessness, and the wretched lackies of the ephemeral, a ravaged eternity wreaks its revenge. A long swig washes down life's boundless mystery and sets what's invisible free.

He grimaces, the grey man, tries in vain to shod his naked foot. His name is Henri, and I'm still taken aback to be lacing his shoe. Another's soul is rarely acknowledged when you're just stumbling about within yourself. Behind a mass of creases and hair, his eyes have the softness of someone who reads your thoughts. I ramble on about the shameful etiquette of indifference, and here I am unsettled by a gentle human gaze. He spits out syllables in fits and starts, talks of his childhood sea, while odd pebbles hunker down inside his pockets. His hot breath flays my face while his cane keeps time.

Henri shows me a pétanque court that's well maintained, and always empty in the morning. I don't know where he got his kit, his new boules shine pridefully in the sun. He used to like his dependable Ricard, but lately he's switched to Quetsche, a formidable ally. It doesn't matter if my aim is just a centimetre off, Henri is a master of sharp ricochets. 12 to 12, my two boules are sent flying, and he wins the point. At the picnic table he roars with laughter at my discomfort, and forces me to take a generous slug of his elixir. The morning breeze dies down while the heat rises, going to our heads. Henri's mind is at rest, he knows that the world's end is in the works today and not tomorrow.

Laid-back souls speak only of survival, between thinking that's chancy or diffident the choice is easy. Henri for his part plumps for the uncertain, his inner freedoms die and revive each day, and faced with the headlong rush of passersby, he's a peevish dropout. One must seize the night, not smother it under a pillow, hold tight to a cryptic, flimsy parchment, because what's essential is always on the brink of extinction. Talk, talk too much, word on word, bold as you can be, season upon season, on the rim of the city's sidewalks. Because the most fated burden is life itself.

He clutches me in his arms as if authentic flesh and bone were something rare. A strange sensation of wet clay. A bad day unlike the others, he gravely declares that he's going to the hospital, never to emerge. No way to learn more, he curses the rain clouds that will flush away the presumed generosity of the local tourists. And there he is, absorbed in tallying a few coins. I'm dismissed for the day.

Morphined, your eyelids shut, your shaved skin a death mask with drool at the lips. I tell you about my childhood's summer nights at Luskville: frogs, ducks, swamp-dwellers and their choir's crescendo. Are your lips moving? Perhaps some trembling at the throat, I think I hear it, I slip the small wooden ball, red, into your right hand, I close your fingers one by one. Go on, toss the jack, let's play one more time. I tell you about the bright cliff under the full moon, the oaks perched there, the rocks sculpted by erosion.

A corpse has the crass capacity to hollow a place out with its silence.

He's gone. An absurd thing to say, but you've got to have something for the ears when a heart stops beating, when the need arrives to loathe all survivors, the assemblage of old, young, ageless, and the smug mien of those for whom immortality is a God-given right. What do they know of that last disaster when the veins bear off the death throes' leavings? Some deaths make us feel that we're running late behind our own.

Droplets in suspension, a heavenly tactile peace, at steeple's height the sky wakes, unfolds. This stellar brightness spans gulfs, touches the eye's depths, is an ardent caress beneath light years. So it is with the dead, their exile's the deepest rooting there is. No remedy for a blessing, no blessing for a cure; our companions beam down light into our open eyes. The beloved face is our most secret cargo, the most far-flung of our journeys.

The Night of the Blind

A wave of heat assaults me just inside the bar. From below my steamed-up glasses I make out musicians in a sweat, and spy a free table near the billiards at the back. I spot naughty slaves, ersatz alcoholics, wizened old souls, and those wired enough to mistake the walls in this lower depth for the inner camber of their skulls. To treat yourself to this circus of libations, just because you can, has implacable logic. I'm privy to the ennui, its wild applause, its standing ovations, its curtain calls.

True nocturnal lovers are hard to find.

Some arrive avid for avatars, moments of fleeting truth rake and claw at intrepid bodies. But mirrors, stealthy, lay down their law, broker the taming of some, the domestication of others; curbed tremors and foiled mutations. The demons deceive us because we cannot deceive them.

I seek out the sorrow in the breach.

The vodka numbs but stops short of stupefaction and it plaits radiant tomorrows, the walking wounded saved, eager to embrace their reclaimed decline. Words with torn sinews call for the dance of life. Words reduced to wounds and blows affirm the defiant ones' worth. Words awash in bitterness flaunt the survivor's pride.

Sand without end runs from my lips.

The dismantling of the world as the bar shuts down, it's closing time for inebriate homebodies, for the crippled, the half-mad, while a few overwrought predators linger, hoping for greater solace. Vast is my hunger during this senseless countdown. I raise myself up, no one any more writes on my bones. I reel through the evening rain, there are drops that fill me with fear and those that confer their blessing.

Night's truth is an armed grenade in the belly's hollow.

The railway line, then at last the viaduct, my viaduct, its stones gone quietly gangrenous beneath their sheen of smug graffiti. I hear scrapings and knocks, the Blind One is there. In childhood my unease swung from fearful to enthralled at the way he sensed my presence. There's nothing you can hide from one who lives in darkness. We have no choice, the sidewalk and I, we close in on his cane as it sweeps, strokes, taps, and outwits perils. He grazes me with a smile.

And he looked up, and said, I see men, I descry like trees walking.

Behind my serried lips I drink in shadows, nothing's less sure than my destination. I turn off towards the quiet side of night and happen on her solitary silhouette. She's sitting on a table in the midst of Pontiac Park, arms folded like wings. Taking in the silence. I slow, walk by, her gaze gives a pitiless sign of life.

A blue cat slips away, its tact matchless as its tread.

I fire up my screen, ready to savour the shared zeal of unhinged anonymity. The flux of pixels makes a merry shambles of my will, I am one with defrocked loners and their clotted vernacular. The jaded world revs up its carousel, an endless, exalted exertion abducts the blind, blissful instant. With the imagined world in thrall, every crease is widened, every fold unfurled. This pornographic mapping blows coldly on the flames.

Submission is mine, but not fulfilment.

The conceit of a grain of sand upon the beach. I have my room, a roof, water, am a bubble in moorage with millions of others, a small bead of froth in the universe. Seeking an exit and finding only an impasse, I huddle under the bedlam of a sheet tensed against the dawn. How long since my tongue dipped itself happily beneath an archway of hips in amorous levitation? I scrape away at my heart with a blade of contrition. Being desolate opens the way to an unbounded indolence.

The floor cracks. Silence affords no gifts. My breathing mimes the echo of something there, drowned thoughts bob ponderously in my breast. My eyelids will not open, insomnia hems and haws, sleep's paresis lays down the law. Fingers scrabble in a maze, let someone lop my head, drop it into a chest, and send it to the bottom of the sea!

Self-contempt shifts no earth, but digs our graves.

Mortal Endeavours

I open a beer and a bag of pretzels to ward off evil spirits. Frozen feet, swollen legs, now a pain in my chest, can't get off the couch, the zapper between my feet, can't reach it, what a strange idea, people being born and dying by the thousands just this instant. A rusted nail lodges in my spine, I try to flee the catastrophe and fall to the floor, claw at the carpet on all fours, pray to whom, pray what, the ceiling light emits a cloud of confetti. A carnivorous flower blooms at the rim of my petrified eye. I crawl towards a feeble light beneath the curtain, my hand flat on my heart.

A voice sets up house in my left ear, it gnaws away quietly at an ice field of viscous ideas. I come back to earth, catch my breath, and my loving steps navigate the neighbourhood, find the viaduct's breach and the crickets' song, poised between valour and death. A white quilt shot through with dark runoffs undoes the memory of birds. Perched on the rampart, my life teeters, graceless, on a porous frontier.

Purity is the first of dreams, the lunatic wish to avenge the unjust and irreparable, all the irreparables. I've never forgotten the clay and its troughs carved out by rain; my mother and I watching from the window the unleashing of the storm, she calmly detailing the world's mysteries. Here I am perched today over a rustling of rust and ash. My hand holds back, my bones shape a curious current of air. A hair's breadth from everlasting stillness.

I've left the top of the viaduct for the entrails below. In the tunnel's bend, I stop just where daylight ends, a blind spot where there is only darkness lapping. A dull tremor grows loud and louder, the engine's eye excites my vertigo. Flat to the wall, transfixed, how many centimetres, how many railcars, which one will squash my body to an ugly pulp? The ponderous lurching of the roar of metal stops at last. Choking, I gulp air as I exit, and myriads of stars fire up at once. I try to snare them but reap only black tears.

For three days I've looked away from the violet riddle on my right leg, an invasive festering obedient to an obdurate law. The wound is worsening, impossible to deny, my flesh consumed, breaking down, the whole calf this morning covered in scales. A taxi bears me away, the sun's glare beats down on the city's windows.

I'm an animal in the making.

One punctures, another spears, the battle is joined to save this leg, and yet time runs slowly through the tubes. I explore this great hectic ship, the hospital, my outings on a stretcher disclose its secret passageways, its half-open doors afford glimpses of raspy breathing and rigid hands. There is death destined only for others, and only for oneself. The cruel equation gives ground, the noise of the living creeps in drop by drop, sickness lifts off one by one my certitudes' weighty stones.

To be stable and in total control of my life: such faith demands enormous energy. My second self is helplessness. A thousand battles cross-hatch my body, trench warfare's being waged in my flesh. The dialogue between gnawer and gnawed is remote from the wider world, this fever is bed-bound, untraveled. An accord between flesh and flesh must plod through downfall and mire. Deep in limbo I laugh, as memory revives.

This incandescent stone in my throat, I don't wake from a nightmare, I labour through it. Arduously I descend a winding staircase, its gummy steps, ancient subterranean waters revive the roots' melancholy and the depths' black blood. I emerge onto a giant dune surrounded by a thousand others, calcified bones to the ends of the earth, red-hot fragments to piece together, a nameless puzzle for a single word.

The stirrings of birds and ferns emerge, a shaded old canal and its ivied locks, I am mad with hope. I find you stretched out on the grass, your arms raised. Your small voice shuts my eyes, under your dress my happy hand. My longing for lavish caresses did not foresee the bite, my arm goes black, my veins burst. Am I a fruit? I grope, the bedside lamp drops to the ground, 2:22, the numbers dance across the floor, hued clouds pulse fiercely in the room, I wait for the storm to pass.

I rise and it's not my room, outside there is a swamp, water lilies, things being born, dying off. I clutch stones to my breast, face-on to the dormant water, the enigma of an unpunished crime, patently committed. I bump up against a chipped bathtub, filthy flakes moulder in the ruined basin, something has crawled, moulted, a beast has fled. I skirt the ghastly empty nest. Down below your silhouette, you enter the river's icy water crying my name, entire suns have time to die before I reach the shore. The eddies cover you over. Then the silence. A splintering in my throat and its immense why.

The man looks me over sternly. Between pubescence and dementia, are there years to be lived? I await his verdict. I launch myself into prayer, with much-loved visions: the sensation of clover under bare feet, an overgrown little cemetery in Portugal, the Irish lighthouse lashed by a high tide, the carved hieroglyphs in the Yucatan, the glass of water and its ice cube in the Brittany sun, the cumulonimbus growling and triumphant, your passing your hand over my head as we watch the storm... The list grows longer, longer still, the judgment comes down, my leg is saved.

Ten minutes of freedom outside while the evening's warmth makes itself felt, mildly unreal. Dark lianas dim the streetlights, trees sigh overhead. A seated man, eyes half-closed, strokes his worn cowboy hat and listens for the miracle, the unseen nighthawk in the dusk's deep blue. Our friend the night speaks softly of beauty's inscrutable transience. I finish my cigarette and regain the elevator, happiness shod in torn slippers. Tomorrow morning I disembark from the great ship of the afflicted. An urn awaits me at home, the long road of deliverance will bear us away.

The urn glows quietly in the window in the light of the sun, after so many years nestled deep in a closet. By its side, a Chinese doll you loved. Thin gold sequins hang here and there from her hair, their trembling as imperceptible as can be. She knows the earth's hidden face. I lift you up, I heft the weight of ashes, this buried state mid-way between atoms and flesh, a truth uninhabitable in its silence. Oblivion is the oldest temple made by man.

To ponder pain and dress its wound was a luxury for years, now the hourglass is empty. *If someone wounds you, don't try to punish him, sit yourself by the river and you'll see his body float by.* That precept of ancient wisdom in no way curbs this new feeling, anger and nostalgia orbit each other, they will dance their way to the birthplace. Luskville is less than three hours by road from Montreal, the time it takes to span eternity. I ready my bags, the urn, and its revenge.

Verticals One

The pack's axiom
Eat, drink, stamp your feet
Humour your desires
Let hours debase hours
Anonymity is no saviour
This skin secured to my bones
Is now inscrutable
Others' eyes at times protest
You're alive, very much alive
On the street in silence
Cannibalism thrives

The rustling of steps in the park
The sneezing of a dog
Its muzzle scouring the ground
What must I search out
I'll never be this dew
With its transient gift of light
A knee to the ground I pick out
A transfigured blade of grass
With poised at its apex
A bead of water stilled
Tell me who I am

On my feet in my own life
I learn to bend down
Home to earth's murmurings
Hear voices and gather them in
A great lost game
Give us a calamity
Grander than happiness
Dying in small doses
Throws light on no one's life

This city sleeps despite the storm
Its sky unredeemably high
The Delphic water of misfortune
Rings round my secret gardens
There is no simple meander
The earth's camber has fled my mind
I must walk for a long time
To get the headwind on my side
I pick up nuggets of ice
They wet the palm of my hand
My thirst welcomes water from the sky

The crime is banal and humdrum
Absence and abstinence join hands
While a languorous arrogance frits away its days
And eye-popping bludgeons just graze my head
All's permitted, while nothing can be done
A hollow barrel in the mouth
The night seeks an explosion
Reaps only the eclipse
The shocks when the days speak false
Just miss their target
Bogus joy is more wearying
Than sorrow

Humans in life's game
Cheat with their lips
Pressed to my restless wounds
That ghostly hour between sweat and dew
What the weeds hide
Revives the frontiers' song
I roam ash-free
To wake not to a jewel in the muck
Nor a fruit you can pick
But to the road's deep-sown seed

Chains dug into the skin
For no reason
Bared entrails convulsed
For no reason
The spiralling down of infirm crazed flotsam
For no reason
The immolated, the tortured, the stoned, the raped
For no reason
Those foundering benumbed on a divan
For no reason
We in the sordid sea
For no reason
I who say we
For no reason

Part 2
The Ashes of Initiation

I live with the constant threat of possession, a constant need to escape from possession, from Control. So the death of Joan brought me into contact with the invader, the Ugly Spirit, and manoeuvred me into a lifelong struggle, in which I have had no choice except to write my way out.

~ William Burroughs

The Return of the Cliff

My childhood home, a jewel invisible from the main road. I loved those red bricks, the same age as the tall trees, the large foundation stones and stones around the windows, the symmetrical openings, the cornice with its rounded dormers. The two chimneys still reign over it all, the tiled terrace thrusts skywards its wrought iron arrows. But inside I find an empty shell that protests at every step. Being an intruder creates an unease impossible to disguise. I shut the urn in behind the cellar door, and go to reclaim the open air.

Here I knew the birds at daybreak, the shadowy swamp, I measured out the summer days with magical tales. Childhood is gone, the wood sleeps, while the dwindling forest endures a waking nightmare, torn between havoc and preservation. But the dawn of the world has never known the story of its birth. I slip on millenary rocks and stumble on a crow's cry; someone breathes, something's at rest, the earth's crust is an open eye beyond feeling and failing.

Red oaks and a few rare white ones greet me on the Eardley escarpment's crest. Facing south, the spot is a haven for rare plants. I hail my red cedar one more time, four hundred years old, unassertive, angled over the void. The roots form elbows bent back to the face of the cliff. The tree is in the world completely, it pays no heed to the abyss and its vertigos. No need to cling to the universe when a rift's enough to keep you alive. I stroke the bark, four hundred years of endurance, ancient cedar, I salute you!

The hours spelled out the days, the minutes spoke the truth, the seconds paraded life before us. The moment is here. The sunset grazes the mineral walls, the earth's flesh bared to light from afar. At my feet, wild apple trees, the swamp, beech trees lost in the middle of the field, the red brick house behind the line of old stripped poplars. I embrace the vista all the way to the banks of the Ottawa River. The hope for a happy stay on earth, a sense of peace, edges me gently towards the rim of the cliff.

The web wafts back and forth at the stream's edge in the bright sun, the spider spins, a rainbow is born. I gather stones, lured by their hues in the running water. Purity is an accident, the union of time and space undoes the murmur of erosion. Blue fruit gleams in the sun, hangs heavy on borrowed time where shades await. I strike a trunk with a stick: better to be found out by a shadow than to catch it unawares. Breaking the silence is an ordeal, reclaiming it is an adventure.

The mysteries of the past will find answers only in the present's endeavours. There is the strident sizzling song of the cicada, there are the hay, the clover, bees, a snake flees, red-winged blackbirds cheep above the reeds. The maples and oaks have long exchanges, I take stock of the ferns' age-old pride and their resolute gentleness. What matures needn't age, everything is older than oneself. I walk, flanked by what's visible and invisible, what more can one ask.

The shadow of a wild rose says its prayer. A ladybug climbs onto my arm, flies off on my breath. The evening breeze awakens an almond tree, I see it as a summons, the earth's deep wisdom with its burgeoning fruits. With a blow from a stone I crack open the shell, bare the almond, the acrid taste tears at my palate, I spit out my act of worship. My mouth has not been pleasured for an eternity, but the scent endures.

I take out my binoculars, I brace myself on my elbows, and point myself straight at the Summer Triangle in the Milky Way: Vega, Altair, Deneb. Within that configuration, I spot Alpha Vulpeculae, a beautiful red giant, in the constellation The Fox. *For as long and as much as the sky will be a question, don't let yourself be distracted by answers.*

The angry ballet of moths around the lantern. They come close to the light, spin madly, most die exhausted long before burning their wings. The very ebbing of our strength stands in the way of our giving voice to our inglorious and unredeemable end. There is little difference between the ephemeral and the eternal, each one leads to a fall.

On the Roads of Pontiac

I leave the Luskville property for the roads of Pontiac. Shawville, Bryson, Campbell's Bay, I head north and stop near Otter Lake, I explore the blasted rocks of the Yates Mine, hemmed in by grass. Thorianite, uranothorite, radioactive minerals once prized, now folded into their false sleep. I hope to find crystals of green apatite, but my prize is a lovely black tourmaline, putting the day's end to bed.

The idea takes shape on a little Black River beach, and in two hours the animal's roughed out. I spend another hour working on its head. Sculpting in sand is near to meditating on meditation. I write in the ground, *The universe is a kernel of pain in the flesh of pleasure.* I know, a twelve-year-old boy will stamp out my words, topple the fox with its pricked-up ears. Before his mother's vacant gaze.

The mist at the Portage-du-Fort dam affords curious pleasures. I think of Ireland, the old ruined lighthouses, steps less and less worn the closer you get to the top. The higher the lighthouse keeper climbs, the more alone he is, free of care and torment. Light is no more an enemy of darkness, it's the dark's adventure. So does the Ottawa River affirm all Immensity, that rootless pride, a beyond that is untranslatable.

These places tell me stories of people from England and Ireland, from France and Poland. In the district of Thorne, I wind my way through what was once Little Germany. Near Ladysmith I go into the Lutheran church that for decades housed German words and songs. There you find the works of Johann Groneau, the mysterious shoemaker-healer, zealous translator of a new bible. The promised land is no more now than a memory entrusted to stone, the cemetery's carved names bravely resist a fateful anonymity. Erasure is also an ending. An old woman lays down flowers next to the stones, the wind doesn't waft me her murmured words, but her luminous smile finds its way.

Does memory only abide far from humans, in the exclusive company of the absent?

Past the village of Litchfield, large overloaded tables come into view in front of a rundown farmhouse. The man waves to me before burying himself again in a magazine as old as everything else. Battered saucepans, cheese graters, coffee-makers, mixers, potato-mashers, chipped cups, toasters, objects shaped by a lifetime's fatigue. Another table is overflowing with handicrafts beyond description, all a man can invent he will concoct to get the better of his solitude, an amalgam of horn and metal, wood and stone, the stuffed animal and the engraved poem. Finally, the perennial board games, an entire battalion of plastic soldiers encircling a one-armed Barbie. Treasures and pointless objects cohabit shamelessly. Five dollars, without bargaining, for three shells and sunglasses from the 1960s. I hold out my bill, his mournful nails purposefully graze my palm. An old yellow dog sighs beneath the chair.

Three young girls hang out beside a decrepit bungalow. The bag's brought out, they inhale the toxic vapours, and reel around between two deep breaths. I know that euphoria, the lightness, the all-powerful feeling behind the feverish desire to flee the world and its memory. They break a window and vanish into the hovel with its mouldering boards. Will they talk of ancient games, will they recall the old woman who told of the earth's birth? An ash-covered mattress awaits them.

We lose our soul ten times, a hundred times in the course of a life, sometimes you have to take it back. Autumn is a good time, a rooting while all flies off. The stream winds its way with its pebbles, its sandy coves, the thick roots of trees with the bent backs of petrified serpents, with its nuggets, its fevers, its dubious foaming, its slanted bushes, an even more slanted birch. And the big rock in the middle. The crossing licks at my calves, the light and stone make a bridge, a thousand and one bridges, insects come and go daintily over the water's mirrorings, it's my turn to be there, to be.

A leaf yellow from among the yellow drops onto my damp shoe. The horizon stops retreating beyond the narrow path, the red maples, the flaming amaranths set to trembling by light alone. This day in October affirms the forest's equinox: the number of leaves on the ground and in the trees has attained its fragile, delicate equilibrium. A magical alphabet gets a bead on beauty. And the moment bears it away.

I wander through the old Moss-Quyon mine, it produced molybdenum during the great wars to strengthen the cannons' steel. Old cement pillars are all resolve and metamorphosis, far from any human salvaging. A toppled wagon, lengths of piping, traces of a road, the orphaned debris of a bygone time now hug the ground's folds. The earth's soul is not vengeful, it will survive us and not judge the consequences of our acts. Matter's slow progress will overtake us all.

Panicked wildfowl scatter as I pass, I find at the end of the path five large stones and their three-thousand-year-old pictograms, perched on the edge of the swamp. *You have to read the water.* Forty years ago those signs conjured a moose whose antlers branched out without end. Today's wind and clouds do not assuage my impatience. I must remain still, not move, think of nothing. Then the luminous dance resumes under an unhoped-for sun, the ochre glitter is reborn on the black water. The roiling mirror throws up an image, a wolf's head swerves by and disappears.

In the Caves of the Kingdom

A dying mouse under my bed, half its body desiccated, only its head moves. Now plunged into a pail of water, the little black eyes go dark. This spectacle unspools my small ration of valour, now with no safe haven. Flee my life? Pain has taught me nothing, nor has healing.

They have failed me, my thousand defences against living too much in the sight of man. Three youngsters cross the property on their ATV, the bobbing mockery of their helmets up against my staved-in fence. As November nears, each night is a bit more fragile than the last. The naked trees are now prey to the bog's stagnant waters, that ceaseless gestation from which one does not wake.

Two men at my door with an air of those in the know, no body odour behind the creases of their shirts, impeccably clean reptiles asserting boldly that I'm a child of their god. Their all-embracing munificence wanes and takes flight at the sight of my gun, which is as fake as their smiles. Another nasty incursion. The house shields me no more, no earthly paradise subsists inside its walls. It's time to pass through the gates to another kingdom, far from the light. The cellar, down below.

The kingdom of misapprehended creatures: mushrooms, wasps, spiders, flies not yet dead, a field mouse never far off. I go to meet a shadow more ancient than the others, the bookcase, a nearly empty piece of furniture in solid wood. One shelf of books survives, along with a globe, a sphere as hollow as a fallen idol. The mountains' contours slip by under my fingertips, a sign that something real has taken flight.

First picture book, the epic of John the Blind. This king of Luxembourg reigned also over Prague and Bohemia, he made war everywhere in Europe until his death in 1346 at the Battle of Crécy, a notorious massacre where the knights, in disarray, bit the dust before the English infantry and archers. The blind king, tied to his horse, charged the enemy, beneath a storm of pikes and arrows, an exploit mad and pointless. On the king's grave, my mother, in secret, laid down flowers in her land's three colours, banned by the Nazis. That picture burned itself into my memory: wounds that never heal teach us to mistrust high-flown words.

Pictures tend to tarry over the gory specifics of martyrdom. To the glorification of passions and miracles I preferred the sad nobility of angels. They gave no thought to the fact that they were improbable creatures, their mission on earth demanded extreme discretion. But the great cosmic dramas are in decline, the exalted giddiness of good and evil is over and done with, an idle angel is one fated to roam an unhinged helpless human world.

In your deportation diary, secured always with a green ribbon, you spoke briefly of the humiliation and horror of the camps. Silesia was but a vast muddy field under a lowering sky, you talked of incognito wanderings in the hills, the company of trees, your coming upon flowers in a clearing. Tenuousness, frugality, the fragile beauty hovering over a teapot, the simple evanescence of the steam. You said the world was not ruled by man.

And that dictionary of Greek mythology, Pandora opening the gift proffered by Zeus, violating the taboo, evil spreading over the earth. It's perhaps worse to await the calamity than to live it. My turn to mine what's lying there. A dried flower appears between Persephone and Poseidon, the gentian gathered during the war, a blue flower from beyond the seas, a sign from beyond the grave.

Why is there Hope at all, freed in extremis from the depths of catastrophe?

Laboured vowels and consonants file by in a scribbler's serried lines till brought up short by a yellowed newspaper clipping. *A woman found in the river dead from drowning*. I couldn't understand how a river could drown. That disaster grown old in obscurity, it's time to drain it to the dregs. I leave the cellar, the first hints of daylight strike the frost on the balcony window. I've always loved placing my fingernail, finger, my whole hand over the frozen arabesques. My brow touches the window and lingers there.

I crave the opaque when the limpid defeats me.

The Soul of the Fox

The screen's granular light jiggles its ghostly snow, judders hypnotically, unfolds the memory lodged in the painting that once hung over the old TV. A woman stretched out on a hillside centres the scene, beyond tall grasses and their tense silhouettes. A lone body is one with the landscape, thanks to the quietude of a face, where the planet's strength is fast bound to tenderness.

A tremor at the bottom of the canvas, there it is again, a patch of colour in the tangle of green shadow. The awful evidence of red fur curled in the grass. The soul of the Fox. Golden threads edge the silky form and unfold in silence the secret calculus of a combat in semi-darkness. I make out its ears. I'm afraid it will raise its head. I'm afraid an image will open its eyes.

The walls around me waver, licked by ancient flames. I clearly feel the Fox entering my pores. With my mother I played a game with a simple candle, our hands patiently shaping shadows from another world. A tiny displacement of the fingers was enough to turn a dog's head into that of a wolf. But our favourite was the Fox. In low voices we conjured an authentic visitation, a felt metamorphosis. A lesson I'd forgotten for too long. Fear's wiles now null and void, the animal, craving trust and steadfastness, bears my thoughts on its breath.

I see myself grabbing a coat, a flashlight, I slip into the moonless night. Thin puckered frost underfoot as far as the car. I pass Shawville, Campbell's Bay, an hour on Route 148; ghostly trees and only Jimi Hendrix for company.

There must be some way out of here, said the joker to the thief
There's too much confusion, I can't get no relief
Businessmen, they drink my wine, plowmen dig my earth,
None of them along the line know what any of it is worth.

I swerve sharply to the right, the Litchfield sign swallowed up already by the night.

Outside in the distance a wildcat did growl,
Two riders were approaching, the wind began to howl.

I recognize the farm and its array of objects piled on tables, a dubious disorder backed by a plaintive sound and its metronomic beat. The strumming stops, starts up again, maybe a bit faster. A glow down there, the man rocking, wrapped in a blanket. The yellow Labrador at his side lifts his clouded eyes my way. A blind dog.

I settle into a torn leather armchair, grab hold of the whiskey bottle sitting on the table. My throat burns. The old man rattles his ice cubes, strokes his earlobe, betrays no uneasiness. He waits. I take another swig, the alcohol's rawness one with my firm resolve. The Fox's soul rolls round in my breast, forces me to talk, falsetto, swallowing my words. *You killed my mother.*

If you are free of anger and hatred, then face your enemy. To stop solitude from gnawing at your bones one by one, to prevent the walls from draining your soul, open yourself to those cherished acts that keep the living alive and the dead dead. I offer no resistance to words that are beyond belief. God sees all, but the devil hears all, so said the elders.

The bottle shatters, I hold the shard to his throat. The man grips my arm, gropes my forehead and cheeks, a hoarse squeal gutters deep in his grey eyes. My hand does its work.

The dog bent over the water bowl, its panting tongue. He'll be hanged from an old apple tree, just like his master. The sordid weight of all those years. The two bodies circle each other slowly, manage to touch, then drift off in opposite directions as if in mutual reproach for the other's existence. I hold out a stick to stop the swaying. The blood has traced arabesques on the ground, the branches of a star fallen to earth.

The river does not speak its name, is a blue embrace charged with stones. My first and last visit to that white fault, all that's lost there, all my doubts flung away like dead wood. I wait until dusk. *Scatter my ashes in the dead of night, near a tall tree.* I cast a silvery smoke, a wordless tribute, into the trees. The stars tremble, you'll have time to study them one by one. The weightless urn, vast as night.

The Fugitive from the Journey

Buddha says that a man hit by an arrow feels two sorts of pain: the rending of his flesh and the rage at having been wounded. We do not embrace events for what they are. Of course vengefulness is born of hatred, a contagion where one evil adds to another, a poison for the soul.

To seek to punish is one thing, to attack impunity is another.

A moist caress renews the vertigo of being where I am. A mist runs down my chest, my hand opens onto a shoulder's white foam. What the skin reports is true, red flecks bloom beneath my nails. What's pressed down and in keeps a watchful eye on the inexpiable wish to live. My bones are on fire, within me a distant nomad land's adrift. You prop up the nape of my neck, abscond with my face, a torrent with its white clouds roars. I hear a limpid language, ecstasy is not ash, but thirst. Real shades have real lips.

A black hole amid the stunning mineral hues. I slip in, it's a simple depression face on to winter. A water drop rolls from the back of the head to the small of the back, that is the grace of this place. The rock deep in the impasse fulfils the promise of this rift. I lay down the dried flower, the blue gentian, an offering to the murmurous earth.

The universe is essentially uninhabitable, and hostile to desires bereft of former lives. A taste of red fruit in my mouth, the mild light-headedness of a traveller on the brink of departure. One last time I gaze on the Luskville cliff, it has always endowed this place with a sense of the beyond. Homesickness is a forgotten art.

Beyond the aircraft's window, fields of secluded trees, roads whose strands trail off, reform, stop short. People sitting in rows are already selecting their films, their primary goal still and always to kill time. Two hours in, the anarchic vista of ice deploys its raw and abstract beauty, faults beckon between Labrador, Baffin Island, Greenland. An implacable slow upheaval slips by under the plane's belly. No one pays heed, the earth is a great vacant mirror.

Verticals Two

The lichen imposes slowness
Time is unmoving
Mist on the blue ice
A fissured tongue of water
Travellers half-formed
Some persevere
Others turn back
You need to be two
The living and the dead

The ground strewn with acorns
Unearth the bare stone
Smelling of shadows
Cast by the sun's hand
I dislodge with a stick
One letter then another
Between drops of rain
My name leaps
Into a studied sea

Ghostly footsteps around the fire
The animals come and go
The song puts down roots
Where the coals sank their teeth
Loyal friends wherever I am
Stranger than flight
Is the bright unreturning sound
Now so faint
I say yes to a bird
Who am I in my listening
The wide world welcomes
Wandering in its beginnings

The still candle
Overturns vases of thought
Drops fall to the white cloth
One after the other
They nibble the shadows
Elsewhere is the silence of here
Snow lightens the trees
Lifts the bark
Translucent fingers cast light
On a longing to live that's more precious than life

Auroras green and pink
Alone the cracking
My frozen breath alone
I reach a strip of snow
Body face on to the sky
Enchanted and swept away
Until the yelping
The rubbing against my leg
The lips pulled back over fangs
The wolf moves quietly off
He's entrusted himself to me
Have I to him?

Those scattered and put to flight
Receive in their flesh
A soft round of breath
Lips bared in desperation
Form a cloud of ashes
Alert to the price of pain
Love is bold as eclipses
The distant captured star
Drunk deep from a well
Smiles on our devotions

What we called silence
Is now our skin
Under our hands silky thorns
Make a liquid murmur
A signature of claws
Slips through the bridal room
Breath lightheaded
The world is the child
The gods will never have
A gulf of tenderness
I caress your voice flung into me
I inhale you in the ancient night
Over snuffed candles
There hovers the vanished light

Das Wandern ist des Müllers Lust,
das Wandern ist des Müllers Lust, das Wandern!
Daß muß ein schlechter Müller sein,
dem niemals fiel das Wandern ein,
dem niemals fiel das Wandern ein, das Wandern.

Vom Wasser haben wirs gelernt,
vom Wasser haben wirs gelernt, vom Wasser;
das hat nicht Ruh bei Tag und Nacht,
ist stets auf Wanderschaft bedacht,
ist stets auf Wanderschaft bedacht, das Wasser.

Das sehn wir auch den Rädern ab,
das sehn wir auch den Rädern ab, den Rädern,
die gar nicht gerne stille stehn
und sich bei Tag nicht müde drehn,
und sich bei Tag nicht müde drehn, die Räder.

Die Steine selbst, so schwer sie sind,
die Steine selbst, so schwer sie sind,
die Steine, sie tanzen mit den
muntern Reih'n und wollen gar noch schneller sein
und wollen gar noch schneller, sein die Steine.

Once, children found sleep in their mothers' voices.

About the Translator

Donald Winkler was born in Winnipeg, graduated from the University of Manitoba, and did graduate study at the Yale School of Drama. From 1967 to 1995 he was a film director and writer at the National Film Board of Canada in Montreal, and since the 1980s, a translator of Quebec literature. In 1994, 2011, and 2013 he won the Governor General's Award for French to English translation, and has been a finalist for the prize on three other occasions. His translation of Samuel Archibald's short story collection, *Arvida,* was a finalist for the 2015 Giller Prize. He lives in Montreal, Quebec.